T0052841

The Fifth Chester Book of Motets
Revised Edition

The Flemish School for 4 voices

Edited by Anthony G. Petti

LIST OF MOTETS

CHESTER MUSIC

Cover:
Virgin and Child in a landscape. Netherlandish School.
Presented by Queen Victoria to the National Gallery
at the Prince Consort's wish in 1863
Reproduced by courtesy of the Trustees,
The National Gallery, London.

HAEC DIES

This is the day the Lord has made: let us be glad and rejoice
in it (*Ps. 117. 24.*).

Jacob Arcadelt (c. 1514–68)

© Copyright 1977, 1989 Chester Music Ltd.

All rights reserved

CRUX FIDELIS

Faithful cross, the one noble tree above all others: none is your equal in foliage,
blossoms or fruit. Dear wood, bearing the dear nails and the sweet burden.

Clemens non Papa (c. 1500 − 56)

GUSTATE ET VIDETE

Taste and see how sweet the Lord is: blessed the man who
trusts in him (*Ps. 33, 9.*).

Henrich Isaac (c. 1450 – 1517)

JERUSALEM SURGE

Rise, Jerusalem, and stand on the heights: and see the joy that
shall come to you from your God (*Bar.5;* 5;*4,* 36.).

Henrich Isaac (c. 1450 – 1517)

AVE MARIA

Hail Mary, full of grace, the Lord is with you, serene virgin. Hail,
whose conception, full of solemn joy, fills the heavens and the earth
with new happiness. Hail, whose nativity was our solemnity and a rising
light like a bright torch, heralded the true sun. Hail blessed humility,
made fruitful without man, whose annunciation was our salvation.
Hail true virginity, spotless chastity, whose purification was our cleansing.
Hail, foremost among all angelic virtues, whose assumption glorified us.
O Mother of God, remember me. Amen.

Josquin des Près (c. 1450 – 1521)

14

TU SOLUS QUI FACIS MIRABILIA

You alone are the worker of miracles, you alone the Creator who made us, you
alone the Saviour who has redeemed us by his most precious blood. To you
alone we fly, in you alone we trust, neither do we adore anyone but you, O Jesus
Christ. To you we offer our prayers: hear what we ask and grant our request,
O good King.

Josquin des Prés (c. 1450 – 1521)

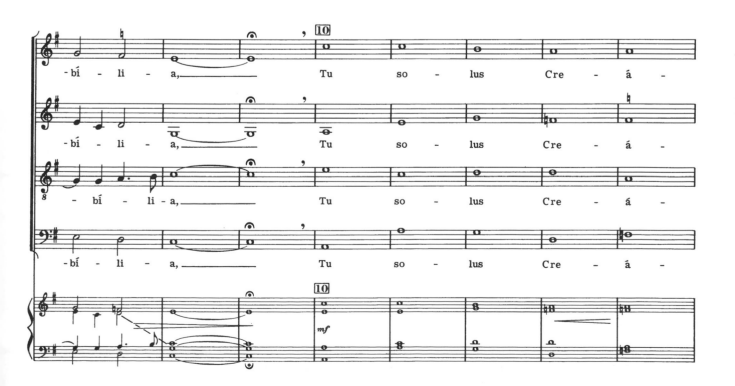

IMPROPERIUM

My heart anticipated reproach and misery; I looked for someone to grieve
with me and there was nobody. I sought one to comfort me and did not
find him; and they gave me gall for food, and for my thirst made me drink
vinegar (*Ps. 68,* **21-2.**).

Orlandus Lassus (1532 – 1594)

JUBILATE DEO.

Let all the earth rejoice in God, serve him with gladness, enter his presence with joy, for the Lord is God indeed (*Ps. 99,* 1-3.).

Orlandus Lassus (1532 – 1594)

SCIO ENIM

I know that my Redeemer lives and that at the last day I shall rise out of the
earth. I shall again be clothed in my body, and in my flesh shall I see God my
Saviour, whom I shall see for myself, my eyes looking upon him and no other.
This is the hope in my breast (*Job. 19. 25-7.*).

Orlandus Lassus (1532 – 1594)

34

O QUAM GLORIOSUM

O how glorious is the kingdom, where all the saints rejoice in Christ.
Dressed in white robes, they follow the Lamb wherever he goes.
Alleluia.

Jacob Vaet (c. 1529 – 1567)

O MAGNUM MYSTERIUM

How great a mystery and how wonderful a sacrament, that beasts
should see the new-born Lord lying in their manger.
Blessed is the Virgin whose body was worthy to bear the
Lord Jesus Christ.

Adrian Willaert (c. 1490 – 1562)

39

EDITOR'S NOTES

The aim of the present series is to make more readily available a comprehensive body of Latin motets from the Renaissance period, combining old favourites with lesser known or hitherto unpublished works. The first five volumes are arranged nationally, covering Italy, England, Spain, Germany and Slavic areas, and the Low Countries, and each contains, on average, twelve motets drawn from not less than six composers. They are for four mixed voices, and should all be within the scope of the reasonably able choir. They also provide a fair selection from the liturgical year, as a guide for the church choir and for performing choirs who like to present their music according to theme or season.

The editor has endeavoured to preserve a balance between a critical and a performing edition. The motets are transposed into the most practical performing keys, are barred, fully underlayed, provided with breathing marks, and have a reduction as a rehearsal aid. Editorial tempi and dynamics are also supplied, but only in the reduction, leaving choirmasters free to select their own in the light of their interpretation of a given piece, vocal resources and the acoustics. The vocal range for all parts is given at the beginning of each motet.

As an aid to musicologists, the motets, wherever possible, are transcribed from the most authoritative source, and the original clefs, signatures and note values are given at the beginning and wherever they change during the course of a piece. Ligatures are indicated by slurs, editorial accidentals are placed above the stave, and the underlay is shown in italics when it expands a ditto sign, or in square brackets when entirely editorial.

Each volume includes a brief introduction concerning the scope of the edition, with notes on the composers, the motets, the sources, editorial emendations and alterations, if any, and a table of use according to the Tridentine Rite.

Though most of the great cultural movements which typify the Renaissance have their origins in Italy, many of the notable musical achievements are Flemish. The Flemings provided much of the impetus for the new forms in music, with Dufay in the vanguard, and their main influence extended well over a hundred years, from the time of Jean Ockeghem, the teacher of Josquin, in the later half of the 15th century, until around the death of Lassus in 1594. Their influence was all the greater because few of the major Flemish composers spent all their lives in their homeland, but travelled widely across Europe, usually being appointed to key positions in royal and ecclesiastical courts. The Italian States in particular welcomed Flemish musicians, and many were employed in the Papel chapel. The present collection contains selections from the work of seven of the most distinguished Flemish composers of the Renaissance period, with prominence given to Josquin and Lassus.

The first composer listed is Jacob Arcadelt (c. 1514-68), whose best-known sacred piece, *Ave Maria*, ironically, was in fact originally a three-part love chanson, and was not set to the Latin words until the 19th century. Arcadelt spent most of his life in Italy, becoming a singer at the Medici court in Florence and then singing-master to the boys of St. Peter's Rome. Although renowned for his secular music, including settings of poems by Michelangelo and Giovanni Guidiccioni's *Il bianco e dolce cigno*, his extant sacred music, though not abundant, is also very impressive. It includes three masses, three sets of lamentations, and a considerable number of motets, some of which survive in manuscript in the Sistine, while others were published in several anthologies such as *Secundus liber . . . Motetti del fiori* 1532. The motets are varied, lively and harmonically interesting, though sometimes lacking the melodic beauty of the madrigals. *Haec dies*, the Arcadelt motet included here, was first published in the volume cited above (copy in British Library) and was reprinted in many other collections in the 16th century. The piece is solemn almost to the point of austerity, with its constant feeling of minor tonality. It begins emphatically with a well-spaced fugue in extended notes, loosely paraphrasing the plainsong melody. The pace quickens for the words of rejoicing, "exsultemus" and "laetemur", and has a slightly jauntier and often dotted rhythm, though still basically in duple time, whereas other composers would have been inclined to move into triple rhythm at this juncture (e.g. Viadana). Certainly, the piece is in marked contrast to Byrd's setting which is in lively dance rhythms almost from the beginning. However, given well-sustained and fullbodied singing, the piece is remarkably effective, as well as being infinitely more subtle than it appears at first sight.

The next composer, Jacobus Clemens non Papa (c. 1500-c. 1566-8) spent more of his life in his native country than did most of his fellow musicians of equivalent stature, though it can be inferred that he spent his early years in Paris. In later life he seems to have resided mainly in Ypres, acquiring the suffix "non Papa" to distinguish him from a fellow townsman, a poet called Jacobus Papa. (It should be noted that the theory that he acquired the title, whimsically or otherwise, to distinguish him from Pope Clement VII is now almost entirely discredited.) Clemens' sacred compositions are not only copious but also very inventive and of a uniformly high standard. The present piece, *Crux fidelis* (transcribed here from the Austrian National Library, Music Collection MS. 19189), was first published in *Liber quartus cantionum sacraum*, 1559. It exhibits many of the characteristic Clemens features, including smoothness and mellifluousness of melodic line, and a sensitive shaping of phrases to fit the contours of the words and their nuances. Another typical aspect is the way in which the motet can be interpreted either modally or in keys, diatonically or chromatically, in accordance with the arcane use of *musica ficta* by the Netherlands composers of the period. Thus, the very timbre of the opening of the motet could be drastically changed by sharping every C and F which is enclosed by D's and G's respectively. Whatever the interpretation of the accidentals, the whole work is a delicate meditation on the cross, intensified by a highly emotive series of climactic repetitions.

With Heinrich Isaac (c. 1450-1517) there is a problem of nationality. He is often claimed to be German, especially since he spent some time at the imperial court of Maximilian, based in Vienna, Constance and in Innsbruck, for which city Isaac wrote the moving valedictory song. But the prevailing opinion is that he was Flemish. Much of Isaac's time was spent in Florence at the court of Lorenzo the Magnificent, where his influence was great, since he was music teacher to Lorenzo's children, who included the future Pope Leo X. Isaac was a master in every prevalent form of vocal music, whether an Italian carnival song, German lieder or sacred polyphony. One of his major achievements is the monumental *Choralis Constantinus*, published long after Isaac's death in three volumes (1550-5), in the first of which the two pieces in this anthology, *Gustate et videte* and *Jerusalem surge*, were published (edited here from the copy in

Uppsala University Library). The three volumes contain over three hundred settings of the Proper for the year and major feasts. In all cases Isaac pays close attention to the plainsong settings, which provide the intonation and framework for the melodic structure. Sometimes the chant appears, in modified form, as the *cantus firmus* in a given line, for example, in the soprano of the *Jerusalem surge*, while the other parts move freely and almost independently of one another. But the *cantus firmus* is also used in a diversity of other ways, for example, fugally or in canon, as in the opening bars of *Gustate et videte*. In both motets a pleasing melismatic undulation is present in all parts, though far less at the expense of the words than in the more gothic compositions prevalent in the late 15th century.

Isaac's exact contemporary, Josquin des Près was universally considered pre-eminent, and acclaimed as "the Prince of Music". He was born in Condé some time between 1440 and 1450, but spent most of his musical life in Italy. For fifteen years he was a chorister in Milan cathedral, followed by a period in the private chapel of Maria Sforza. He was a member of the Sistine chapel from 1486-99, and then, after revisiting Milan and going to Ferrara, he returned to his birthplace, where he became a canon of the cathedral. He died in or around 1521.

Josquin was the most imaginative of his musical contemporaries, and always strove to ensure that his works were organic compositions conveying with acute sensibility the emotional, intellectual and descriptive connotations of each section of his text, though not in the more obviously extravert way of many composers of the High Renaissance and Early Baroque periods. The contrast of styles in his music can often be staggering, especially if one compares the frisky little onomatopoeic song of the cricket, *El grillo*, with the serene majesty and deep devotion of his *Missa de beata virgine*. Josquin's output includes about seventy-five secular works, around twenty masses and a hundred motets. It is mainly in his motets that his greatest achievements and the strongest imprint of his individuality are to be found.

Probably the most famous of his motets is his four-part *Ave Maria*, one of three extant settings by Josquin. This survives in several contemporary manuscript copies, though at least one of them, that in the former Preussische Staatsbibliothek (MS. 40013), was destroyed during the Second World War. It was also published by Petrucci in *Motetti a numero trentatre* (editions in 1502 and 1504). The motet is a setting of one of the innumerable hymns to the Virgin that open with the angelical salutation. In this case the text (which varies from manuscript to manuscript quite considerably) comprises five quatrains, all but the first in tetrameters rhyming aabb, followed by a concluding couplet and amen. Each stanza is given its own distinctive melodic phrase, rhythmic grouping and disposition of voices, and in most cases, final cadence. However, the result is not one of fragmentation but of counterbalance, continuity and growth, coupled with a sense of surprise and illumination, when a new section flowers into a completely different rhythm, movement and harmonic texture. Josquin gives the motet a generous sense of space and time, and uses translucent harmonies. He is very sparing in his vocal resources. The employment of all four parts is reserved mainly for the close of stanzas, the final invocation, and for the musical highlight, "Ave vera virginitas" (which is often abstracted and sung as a separate motet). The opening of the *Ave Maria* is a delicate musical filigree with a systematic, barely overlapping canon moving from the highest to the lowest voice. The pace is measured and gentle with melismas confined mainly to the last words of each line. The second stanza (bar 31ff.) begins with a duet in the upper voices answered by three lower voices, all parts coming together to express the idea of filling earth and heaven with joy. The next two stanzas are again antiphonal, upper voices being answered by lower voices. The texture falls away almost to nothing, with a bare octave at the cadence (bar 94), and then suddenly, for the fourth stanza, the most sustained section of four-part writing in the motet is introduced in quick triple time. It is almost homophonic but for the subtle syncopation of the tenor, which sings in canon at the fifth with the soprano, only one note behind, providing a remarkable effect of contrasting triple and duple rhythms between the parts.

For the last stanza Josquin returns to antiphonal effects, but in a consciously asymmetrical way and with a considerable amount of syncopation. The final invocation, clearly detached from the body of the work by a bar's rest, is an entirely homophonic utterance in lengthened notes, with the simplest chordal progressions, alternating mainly between tonic and dominant, and ending with a bare fifth on extended repeated notes for the Amen.

The second Josquin motet, *Tu solus*, the first part of a double motet published in Petrucci, *Motetti de Passione*, 1503, has even greater harmonic simplicity than the *Ave Maria*, and is far more compact. The writing is mainly homophonic and dwells virtually on every syllable by the prevalant use of the breve and frequent *fermata*, so that the effect is of profound and sonorous meditation. However, Josquin introduces stylistic variation in the two final sections of the work, forestalling the possibility of monotony. At bar 40 there is antiphony, much as in the *Ave Maria*, but beginning with the lower rather than the upper voices, and continuing instead of repeating the verbal text. All voices come together symbolically for "nec alium adoramus" and for the Holy Name (bars 47-54). The last section begins, as the preceding one, with a pair of lower voices, but progresses to three and then four for the concluding vocative, "Rex benigne", in which every syllable has a *fermata* or its equivalent.

Orlandus Lassus (1532-94) is known by various forms of his name, including the Italian and Flemish versions, Orlando di Lasso and Orlande de Lattre. He probably began as a choirboy in his birthplace, Mons. Melodramatically, he was kidnapped on account of his beautiful voice and spirited off to Italy, where he soon entered the service of Ferdinand Gonzaga, and travelled widely, visiting Palermo, Naples and Milan. At twenty one he became choirmaster at St. John Lateran in Rome, but held the post only two years, returning to the Low Countries. After periods of travel in northern Europe, he was employed by the Duke of Bavaria in 1556, and remained attached to the Bavarian court for the rest of his life, though he was a frequent honoured guest in many capitals of Europe.

An extremely prolific composer, with well over 1,200 works to his credit (including five hundred motets), Lassus displays an extraordinary mastery of all forms and styles of vocal music current in his day. It is hard to believe, for example, that the extravert and ribald madrigal, *Matona mia cara*, the delicate French love song, *Mon coeur se recommande à vous*, and the highly chromatic and etherial *Prophetiae sibyllarum*, each masterpieces in their own genre, all stem from the same pen. There are, however, a few places where Lassus appears to nod, or where the polyphony is a little dense. Some of his shorter masses are too utilitarian and brief, paying little attention to the syllabication or nuances of the words; and some of his motets are a little remote or too austere. But these observations are subjective, and scarcely can detract from the universal admiration which, then as now, caused him to be considered the greatest of the Renaissance Flemings.

The three pieces selected here indicate some of the range of expression and styles Lassus was capable of in his four-part motets. The first two, *Improperium* and *Jubilate Deo* have been edited here from the *Magnum opus musicum*, 1604, though they were first published in 1585. The *Improperium* is a very sensitive portrayal of the suffering of Christ on the cross as foreshadowed in Psalm 68. Set mainly in the Aeolian mode, though more properly in D minor (transposed here to E minor), it opens with a slow fugue with an almost painful ascent in the angular *stretto* dialogue of soprano and alto. The opening phrase is imitated three times with gathering intensity as all parts enter, the little ornamental cadences which recur for "meum" almost adding to the anguish rather than palliating it. The succeeding phrase for "miseriam" expresses misery in divers ways in each part: the almost jerky syncopation of the soprano; the awkward third and the cadence in the alto; the series of three runs in the tenor connoting an outcry of pain, and the groaning pedal point in the bass. The next section, "et sustinui" shatters expectations by beginning not with an E minor tonic chord to follow the half close, but on a D major chord. This supposedly sounds an optimistic note for "et sustinui", quickly to be destroyed by the consistent cancelling of the F sharp, which changes the D major to minor; and the final cadence of this section is left in an agony of uncertainty (bars 27-8). The mood quietens for "consolantem" with the lower and upper voices singing the same phrase antiphonally, but with all voices combining for "et non inveni". The descending passages for "et dederunt" begin in upper voices and, as in the preceding section, grow in intensity by the addition of the other voices, a series of suspensions, and the application of the F natural yet again. The "et in siti" is the most poignant section, with the heart-searing sequence of rising fourths. Thereafter, the piece moves gradually to rest, but the acidity of "aceto" is nevertheless conveyed by the alternation of accidentals and the final Phrygian cadence.

The second motet, *Jubilate Deo* mainly in the bright Ionian mode, is a breathtaking *tour de force*, sustaining its impetus from beginning to end, and culminating in a shout of joy and triumph. The opening fugue, vigorous and emphatic, is repeated in the upper parts with slight variations (a common Lassus feature) but soon gives way to the cross-rhythms of a second and even quicker paced fugue with a very gymnastic melismatic tenor line (bars 11ff.). This section quietens somewhat for "laetitia" and closes on a bare fifth (bar 21), to be succeeded by emphatic imperatives in rising thirds for "Intrate" and a remarkably angular almost monosyllabic "in conspectu eius", with no coincidence of syllables among the voices, as if they had literally entered the sacred presence from different directions, though they all come together for "exsultatione" (bars 25-7). A relatively smooth *stretto* fugue follows for "quia Dominus", though with the tenor always a step ahead. Finally, a fourfold sequence of phrases for "ipse est Deus" leads to a magnificent climax as each voice moves to the top of its register for the concluding percussive acclamation.

Among the most remarkable of Lassus' sacred works are two sets of lessons from the *Book of Job*, published in 1565 and 1582. *Scio enim* comes from the first set, being the third part of the motet, *Pelli meae consumptis carnibus* (edited here from the British Library copy). Like Josquin, Lassus gives each section its own distinctive entity, though linking it to the next with artistic inevitability. The motet begins in the Ionian mode (or more properly C major, transposed here to Eb major), but goes through many vicissitudes, with rapid alternation of major and minor chords, until the final hopeful though somewhat ambiguous Phrygian cadence. The opening is a vigorous brief canon between the tenor and bass, containing a very affirmative melisma for "enim". It is succeeded by all four parts singing mainly at the top of their registers for "Redemptor", the entry of the soprano being as strikingly effective as it is unorthodox in the period. A considerable amount of word-painting follows in the next sections: the third of the chord is raised to A♮ for "novissimo die", there are leaps in each part of an octave or a fifth for "surrecturus", and a sudden mystical Db major chord for "Deum". The texture changes to antiphonal two-part fugue for "Quem visurus", moving into four-part homophony in almost *falsobordone* style for the remainder of the piece, with touches of apocalyptic visions in the juxtaposing of C minor and D major chords, followed by G major and F major (bars 46-50).

Jacob Vaet (c. 1529-67) is one of the lesser lights, but nevertheless a very accomplished composer. He was choirmaster to Maximilian, king of Boehmia, and from 1564 to 1567 kapellmeister in Vienna under the patronage of the Emperor. The output of Vaet is somewhat modest by comparison with that of his contemporaries, and consists almost entirely of sacred music, including nine masses, six magnificats, and seventy-six motets mostly for five and six voices. The motets are enterprising and lively and show an acute response to verbal rhythms.

The *O quam gloriosum* (University of Tübingen MS 40028) is vigorous and has a lively sense of pace. The opening fugue has an interesting counter-balance of a lively (if somewhat fussy) melodic line against the minor tonality of the Aeolian mode, with the raised B at cadences giving the impression of C minor (transposed here from the original A minor). The succeeding sections are similar to those of the Victoria setting, which it predates. For example, "in quo cum" is monosyllabic and fugal; "gaudent" has ascending melismas; "omnes sancti" is treated homophonically in lengthened notes and repeated for emphasis; and "amicti stolis" has the identical rhythm to Victoria's, including the dotted crotchet. Thereafter, the similarity ends. A simple rising progression is used in most parts from "et sequuntur" to "Agnum", and then the otherwise smooth flow of the motet changes to broken phrases, with quaver rests for "quocumque". Finally, there is an extended and florid run of alleluias (bars 43-49), which is repeated and ends in a triumphant F major chord.

The last composer represented in this collection, Adrian Willaert (c. 1490-1562), had a great reputation as a musician and composer in his time, being hailed as the new Josquin, but he still awaits a convincing revival today. He travelled widely in Italy, and then entered the service of King Lewis of Bohemia. When the king died in 1526, Willaert returned to Italy and became master of the music at St. Mark's, Venice, remaining in office there for thirty-five years, though he returned to the Low Countries from time to time. Among his many contributions to the new style of music are his consistent principles of matching the music to the words and in perfecting the declamatory style. Willaert's output includes madrigals and canzoni, ricercari, psalms, hymns, masses and a Magnificat. His fame in sacred music rests mainly now on his motets, of which *O magnum mysterium* is a good though not especially characteristic example. The first part of a double motet, it was first published in *Musica quatuor vocum, liber secundus*, 1539, and reprinted in the second edition of *Musica quatuor vocum liber primus*, 1545, from which the present edition has been taken (copy in the British Library). Even though the settings of the *O magnum mysterium* by Byrd and Victoria are better known, Willaert's version is worthy to be in their company. It does not contain their intensity or feeling of awe, but has a beauty and inventiveness of melodic line, and a wonderful sense of structural integration. The mood is one of unalloyed but quietly contained joy, from the slowly unfolding rising opening, through the gentle undulation of "in praesepio", to the final reverential melismas for the Holy Name. It should be noted, too, that Willaert uses many of the note values, rhythms and syncopations that Victoria was to employ in his setting, and often the same technique of contrasting upper and lower voices, as in "viderent Dominum natum"; but these examples are surely a case of great composers thinking alike.

Table of use according to the Tridentine rite

Motet	liturgical source	seasonal and festal use
Haec dies	2nd ant. Vespers; beginning, Gradual, Easter	Easter
Crux fidelis	Reproaches, Good Friday	Lent and Passiontide, Feasts of Cross
Gustate et videte	Communion, 8th Sunday after Pentecost	Communion, general
Jerusalem surge	Communion, 2nd Sunday of Advent	Advent
Ave Maria	Composite hymn and sequence	Blessed Virgin
Tu solus	Hymn to Christ (mixed with vernacular)	Christ, Passiontide, general
Improperium	Offertory, Palm Sunday	Passiontide, Lent
Jubilate Deo	Offertory, Sunday within octave of Epiphany	Christmas, Epiphany, general
Scio enim	Lesson VIII, Office of Dead	Funerals, Easter, general
O quam gloriosum	Magnificat ant., All Saints	All Saints, general
O magnum mysterium	4th respons., Matins of Christmas	Christmas, Epiphany